The Contaminated Rooms

In a Sanctified House

The Courtroom of Heaven: Know your Legal Rights!

Apostle Israel Peña

The Stairways to Heaven Enterprise Inc.

Scriptures noted (NKJV) are taken from the *New King James Version* ®. Copyright © 1982 by Thomas Nelson. Used by permission. Scripture quotations marked (NIV) are from the *Holy Bible, New International Version* ®, NIV® Copyright © 1973, 1978, 1984, 2011 by Biblica, Inc.® Used by permission. All rights reserved worldwide. Scripture quotations marked (NLT) are taken from the *Holy Bible, New Living Translation*, copyright ©1996, 2004, 2007, 2013, 2015 by Tyndale House Foundation. Used by permission of Tyndale House Publishers, Inc., Carol Stream, Illinois 60188. All rights reserved.

Published by Create Space an Amazon Company www.Createspace.com printed in the United States, France, Germany, United Kingdom, Spain and Italy.

Library of Congress Cataloging-in-Publication
ISBN-13: 978-1537126791
ISBN-10: 1537126792
Cover Design: Miguel Blanco

Editorial House: The Stairways to Heaven Enterprise Inc.
www.TheStairwaysToHeaven.com

Title also available in Spanish:
Las Habitaciones Contaminadas: En una casa Santificada

Contents

Acknowledgments

First, I would like to thank my Lord and Savior Jesus the Christ, who has never failed me. By way of His Holy Spirit He has given me these revelations to share freely.

I would like to thank my beautiful wife Prophetess Dalimar Peña, who has in these last years of restoration been a truly virtuous woman of God who edifies her household.

I would like to thank my daughters for being such an inspiration; they have allowed me to see why it is so important to preach the gospel of freedom.

I also want to thank my family both physical and spiritual for always showing me the support necessary in and out of season. Thank you FLOW Kingdom Ministries for believing in me, but mostly for believing in God.

Introduction

In 2005, the Lord introduced me to what I believe is the most important part of ministry, Deliverance. My heart for the souls has always been paramount. Early in the ministry of Deliverance, I understood how to love and be compassionate. Throughout the years, I know I have been involved in more than 2,000 one-on-one deliverances. The levels of appreciation expressed has demonstrated the hunger that is out there for inner healing. This ministry Jesus introduced for the first time on this planet, is the one least taken into account, but I thank God for choosing this temple to be one of the many epicenters of this ministry that focuses on internal sicknesses.

My life is not my own. The sense of urgency I feel to heal souls, takes a large toll. However, as long as I keep

Him first, He will grant me the strength to conduct deliverance, and teach others to do the same. Power comes by revelation, revelation comes by relationship, and relationship comes by surrender. So Lord, I surrender. Amen.

Chapter I

Compassion

According to (Psalm 145:8-9 NLT), "The LORD is merciful and compassionate, slow to get angry and filled with unfailing love. The LORD is good to everyone. He showers compassion on all his creation." These verses show that God doesn't say "all His children," rather "all creation." So, all of His creation partakes of His compassion. That's why even when an animal is in a state of distress or in need, we feel this urgency to tend to them. When Jesus showed up on the scene, He literally came in and established a kingdom of compassion against a kingdom of earthly passion. He expressed His authority and the things that were there had to react even without Him saying a word. His light invaded the darkness and the darkness had to react. The kingdom concept is to dominate by way of the king's dominion. Jesus chose to come during the Roman Empire because He wanted them to understand the concept of conquering and occupying in the spirit. There is something about an invasion that when it takes place, there is an entering into territory and taking control of it. You don't just win by entering, you win by entering and taking control. That's what our King did. He brought the Kingdom back into full effect.

If your influence is as strong as Jesus' was, you don't have to be so close because your circle of influence or cipher will affect the people around you. Jesus allowed people to enter His circle of influence and it caused the kingdom to affect them. This has everything to do with deliverance. Being compassionate is vital. If there is no compassion there is no power.

As shown in (Mark 1:40-41 NIV), the question is not whether Jesus is willing to heal. He does want to heal: "A man with leprosy came to him and begged him on his knees, 'If you are willing, you can make me clean.' Jesus was indignant. He reached out his hand and touched the man. 'I am willing,' he said. 'Be clean!'" When praying, there is no need to beg because we are not beggars. We are sons and daughters of the One True God, of a King. That means we are royalty. Now we have answered the question of whether or not He is willing.

God is not interested in juggling your Sins

In (Micah 7:7-9 NIV) we learn that God is not interested in juggling your sins: "But as for me, I watch in hope for the LORD, I wait for God my Savior; my God will hear me. Do not gloat over me, my enemy! Though I have fallen, I will rise. Though I sit in darkness, the LORD will be my light. Because I have sinned against him, I will bear the LORD's wrath, until he pleads my case and upholds my cause. He will bring me out into the light; I will see his righteousness."

God already placed the punishment on His son. Jesus took on all of our sins so that all of it would be nailed on the cross: all sickness, disease, mental issues, and all internal upheaval. When He died, its power to infiltrate our temples died too. Therefore, we live in a real or true world; you must understand the difference. To move in deliverance, you must know that the person is really sick but truthfully is not. What I am trying to explain is the person is *really* bound, but the *truth* is the person is not. In order to understand this you must know the difference between *reality* and *truth*. The devil is a liar who uses reality to make you think something that you should not because when Jesus died, His truth prevailed over reality.

Jesus kept saying, I tell you the truth. Hence, the reason why there is a continuous conflict between that which is real and that which is true. Reality and truth are always conflicting. One example of a real and true situation is when Jesus walked on the water. The real says that it is impossible to walk on water, but it truthfully can be done. The truth is always able to alter what we feel is the reality.

Chapter 2

What is the Anointing?

The Book of (I Samuel 5:1-7 NLT) helps us further understand the expression "power by way of compassion" as first we see what the "anointing" is:

> After the Philistines captured the Ark of God, they took it from the battleground at Ebenezer to the town of Ashdod. They carried the Ark of God into the temple of Dagon and placed it beside an idol of Dagon. But when the citizens of Ashdod went to see it the next morning, Dagon had fallen with his face to the ground in front of the Ark of the LORD! So they took Dagon and put him in his place again. But the next morning the same thing happened—Dagon had fallen face down before the Ark of the LORD again. This time his head and hands had broken off and were lying in the doorway. Only the trunk of his body was left intact. That is why to this day neither the priests of Dagon nor anyone who enters the temple of Dagon in Ashdod will step on its threshold. Then the LORD's heavy hand struck the people of Ashdod and the nearby villages with a plague of tumors. When the people realized what was happening, they cried out, "We can't keep the Ark of the God of Israel here any longer! He is against us! We will all be destroyed along with Dagon, our god."

When the anointing shows up, it reveals that which is imperfect. On top of that, it takes action against that which is unauthorized. The ark is a representation of the anointing and if you pay attention, you see that the anointing causes discomfort when external entities are not aligned. Their response to the ark in the temple was predicated upon how much havoc was caused when it was originally brought in.

When the anointing shows up, things start to shift and when things aren't right, things get destroyed. The statue fell face down almost in a form of worship. They tried to put it back up again, but this time God made it clear that He will eliminate both areas that are of communication: the hands and the head. In (2 Samuel 6:1-7), we are able to witness when the anointing is in the right place, worship becomes authentic. In verse 5, they were worshipping, but in verse 6 it is clear that it is detrimental to attempt a change from the original design or format established by God. In other words, don't switch the program unless it's given to you by God. In verse 7, the anointing could kill when you are unauthorized to move in it. The anointing is the power of Holy Spirit and even a piece of cloth could absorb the anointing.

The Anointing is Transferable

In (Acts 19:11-12 NKJV), we learn that Paul took handkerchiefs, laid his hands on them, gave them out, and everyone who touched them was healed and delivered. "Now God worked unusual miracles by the hands of Paul, so that even handkerchiefs or aprons were brought from his body to the sick, and the diseases left them and the evil spirits went out of them."

If we also take a look at (Ezekiel 44:17-19 NLT),

we find a Levitical priesthood through the family of Zadok

that were given the role of blessing the people, but were told

to remove their clothes so not to endanger anyone by

transmitting holiness to them through their clothes:

> "When they enter the gateway to the inner courtyard, they must wear only linen clothing. They must wear no wool while on duty in the inner courtyard or in the Temple itself. They must wear linen turbans and linen undergarments. They must not wear anything that would cause them to perspire. When they return to the outer courtyard where the people are, they must take off the clothes they wear while ministering to me. They must leave them in the sacred rooms and put on other clothes so they do not endanger anyone by transmitting holiness to them through this clothing."

This demonstrates how even a good thing

administered at the wrong time can endanger those who are

in the midst. When Jesus gave himself as the ultimate sacrifice it did not change the power of transference, but it gave authority to those who would have normally been unauthorized before the cross.

That means that not just anyone can lay hands on you or impart upon your life. If it is done out of season, it can cause a damaging ripple effect even if it is done with good intentions. So, what happens is that when someone who is anointed lays hands on a vessel "person," there is a level of power that is given. If the timing is off, that vessel can burst because it is not able to contain the level of anointing that is being distributed. Jesus mentions this when He referred to old wineskin that is being filled with new wine. The consequence of that is spilled wine because an old wineskin will eventually burst. That is why the anointing can either bless you in abundance or cleanse you, which may hurt in the process. The reason why it would hurt is because there are parts of you that have been connected to you for a long time that needs to be amputated.

Chapter 3

The Power of the Anointing

In (2 Kings 13:20-21 NLT), we see the power of the anointing: "Then Elisha died and was buried. Groups of Moabite raiders used to invade the land each spring. Once when some Israelites were burying a man, they spied a band of these raiders. So they hastily threw the corpse into the tomb of Elisha and fled. But as soon as the body touched Elisha's bones, the dead man revived and jumped to his feet!" In verse 21, we see that Elisha was so anointed that even after he died, the anointing remained on his bones. The story is about a group of men, who in their rush threw a dead man's body into the tomb of Elisha. When the body touched the bones, the man resurrected.

Paul did things in the Book of Acts like healing people with a cloth. That was not found in the Old Testament. Since the New Testament, during the time when

Paul was doing this, these miracles did not exist. His reference point would have been the existing Scriptures. He thought outside of the box and did something that was never done before. Holy Spirit is always working, even when we don't understand what is being done.

Those who say, "If it is not in the Word, it cannot be used or done", would conclude that Paul was wrong because he moved in a miracle that was not in the Word during his time. They did not have motor vehicles or aircrafts back in biblical times. Although you will not find it in the Word, we know that miracles today can occur in a car and on a plane. It is obvious that today, with all the high levels of technology there are many unusual miracles that have no biblical reference point. You can do a miracle through the

Internet, television, and radio. Just because it is not in the Word, does not mean it can't happen.

When Paul wrote the letter to the churches, he had no idea that it was going to end up as Scripture. He was just doing what we would call a "Facebook Message", because that was Facebook back then. When he wrote what we are now able to read in (2 Timothy 3:16 NIV), he had no idea that it would be part of the 66 books of the canon: "All Scripture is God-breathed and is useful for teaching, rebuking, correcting and training in righteousness..."

When he said, all Scripture is inspired by God, he had no idea they would put his epistles in the same category. In order to comprehend this, you must have a mindset aligned with revelation. When Paul received a revelation, he wrote it and gave it to different churches. All he was getting was brand new information for that season. It was not until

300 years later that it was included in the Word and

approved in the First Council of Nicaea 325 AD.

Chapter 4

The Anointing and Deliverance

There are a combination of things in deliverance that are experienced. In (Galatians 5:19-21 NLT), we find that Paul is dealing with believers. Every letter Paul wrote was to the church.

> "When you follow the desires of your sinful nature, the results are very clear... sexual immorality, impurity, lustful pleasures, idolatry, sorcery, hostility, quarreling, jealousy, outbursts of anger, selfish ambition, dissension, division, envy, drunkenness, wild parties, and other sins like these. Let me tell you again, as I have before, that anyone living that sort of life will not inherit the Kingdom of God."

A Christian can have an unauthorized inhabitant in a room that is still contaminated. You can accept the truth of salvation but reject the truth of deliverance. In other words, you are heaven bound while living in hell. Therefore, you are good with your passport to heaven meanwhile living a life of torment, depression, anxiety, hate, unforgiveness, and addiction. This does not mean that you do not love Jesus; it means that you do not fully trust Him.

An Out of Season Word

In (Acts 16:16 NIV), we read about a female slave who had a spirit by which she predicted the future: "Once when we were going to the place of prayer, we were met by a female slave who had a spirit by which she predicted the future. She earned a great deal of money for her owners by fortune-telling."

The demon that was inside of her was speaking an annoying truth out of time, which could be more damaging than a lie. It was true that Paul was a servant of the Most High God. Paul became exasperated.

He was tired of hearing the same thing repeatedly: although it was a truth, she was not supposed to keep saying it, so it was tormenting his spirit.

This woman was annoying. She was saying something that was true while simultaneously bothering Paul's spirit. The reason why he was bothered was not because she was telling a lie, but rather the constant repetition that was not in sequence with God's divine order. In other words, she spoke a truth in an untimely fashion. Today, in the prophetic, you have people that receive a word from God, but give birth to it prematurely, turning it into an abortion. Anything delivered before time does not have all of its organs in place in order to function accordingly.

Paul and Silas in Prison

There is a way for one to receive freedom and it is by being around those who worship in spirit and in truth. While Paul and Silas were in prison, they began to praise and worship. The anointing that was caused by this combination of the apostolic and the prophetic allowed a breakthrough not just for them, but also for every prisoner that was in close proximity.

Their freedom was based on being around true worshippers. Why should I go to church? Because you might end up with a true worshipper around you. The other person who has mastered worshipping God may end up freeing you. There is a phrase that is used when conducting deliverance: "The deliverer gets delivered." While you are conducting deliverance, there are things in you that are being cleaned out simultaneously. Being bound is not a good feeling. It prevents you from doing God's will, and being who you really are in Jesus. People often do things at times not because they want to, but because they are influenced to and it eventually becomes a sickness.

An example of this is the minister who comes to church with a great message for the people. Afterwards, he goes home at night and opens up the computer which grants him access to the Internet. While no one is looking, he begins to entertain the room in his soul that is still contaminated. He desires to serve God, but the sickness of perversion dominates his alone time.

Chapter 5

The Contaminated House

In (Leviticus 14:33-36 NKJV) we read:

> And the LORD spoke to Moses and Aaron, saying:
> "When you have come into the land of Canaan, which
> I give you as a possession, and I put the leprous plague
> in a house in the land of your possession, and he who
> owns the house comes and tells the priest, saying, 'It
> seems to me that there is some plague in the house,'
> then the priest shall command that they empty the
> house, before the priest goes into it to examine the
> plague, that all that is in the house may not be made
> unclean; and afterward the priest shall go in to
> examine the house.'"

We are houses. Jesus said we are living temples. What

happens when the temple of God is invaded? What is the

reaction Jesus had when He went to the house of God and

there were things going on that should not have been? He

started turning over tables: "Then, going over to the people

who sold doves, he told them, 'Get these things out of here.

Stop turning my Father's house into a marketplace!'" (John

2:16 NLT). That is how He feels about a contaminated house. When Jesus expressed His intense disgust in John 2:16 and Mark 11:15, that was a demonstration of how He feels about His temple "us" being contaminated. Some scholars believe the anger expressed was towards the actual physical Temple located in Jerusalem.

Jesus Establishes a Case Law

The real reason Jesus did what He did, was to establish a case law. During a deliverance, we can speak of how He enters into the temple, (which is the person), and vigorously cleans it out. The hands of man no longer build the temple, but rather, we are the living temples of the living God.

Today, many people of faith focus more on the altar in the church rather than the altar in the heart. They would rather keep the church clean, but leave the heart dirty. No longer is there a temple with an altar because when the veil ripped in two, the power of the altar was transferred to our hearts.

If there is one thing that gets Jesus upset, it is when a house is contaminated. He is not concerned about "the place" anymore. He is concerned about "you!" When you are a house of God, you let the property owner into the house to do repairs. The property owner goes in and asks, "What's wrong?" and you reply, "I have a bunch of roaches, I need an extermination because one of my rooms is contaminated. It has a roach infestation." If that room remains closed and unattended, the infestation grows and starts affecting the other rooms.

The contaminated house causes the person to go to the high priest, as referred to in the Old Testament. This sounds like John 9. We learn about a man who was born blind and many thought that it was due to a family generational curse. Jesus explained that no one was at fault of sin but rather, this man was blind so that he could receive the miracle of seeing from God and give God the glory.

The example found in Leviticus 14:33-36 is about a contaminated house that required inspection to see if the mildew was not just external, but also internal. If that was the case, it had to be removed. When removed, the contaminants were taken to a place where all things that are decrepit would be taken.

In the removal of contamination, one of the key elements of keeping it from being contaminated again is filling up the room. Leaving it empty creates a problem because something else comes to fill in the space: "And when he comes, he finds it swept and put in order. Then he goes and takes with him seven other spirits more wicked than himself, and they enter and dwell there; and the last state of that man is worse than the first" (Luke 11:25-26 NKJV).

The type of appliance and how much power is pulled in by that appliance, determines what type of plug you need. If there is a need for a lot of power, then the plug needs to be thick. If it's just a little bit of power, the wire can be standard. When Jesus came down the mountain with His three disciples after the Transfiguration, a man went to Him and told Him that His disciples were trying to cast out demons from his son but were unsuccessful. Serious mildew requires serious equipment. Your anointing may be a standard plug anointing or it can be a thick plug anointing. Depending on how thick your wire is, is how much anointing can flow through you.

Standard Plug and Thicker Plug Anointing

This goes back to what I mentioned earlier about new wineskin and old wineskin. The old wineskin's walls are too thin to keep and contain new wine. It requires a wineskin with thicker walls, and newer fabric. To further understand how you can receive a revelation, the wineskin would be your paradigm. What you believe and what is revealed to you, determines how much power you exude: which is the wine.

If you do not Receive Revelation: No Elevation, No Power

Contamination is as simple as connection. Someone unauthorized touching your head can be as detrimental as someone taking a bat and swinging it on your head. Why did Jesus go to the Cross? What was He trying to fulfill? When it comes to the Cross of Jesus Christ, the whole scenario had to be equivalent to what the high priest did to purify a contaminated house. At the Cross Jesus had to fulfill the purification process of the contaminated houses.

In (Leviticus 14:49-53), it was required to take two birds, so Jesus took two thieves. A cedar stick was also required, and in place of that, was the cross. His garment replaced the scarlet yarn. The hyssop branch (sponge with vinegar), was used when He requested something to drink.

Jesus being the ultimate priest, used all the elements required to declare all the houses "us", to no longer be contaminated.

When it comes to the Cross of Jesus Christ, the whole scene had to be set up that way. If one thing would have been out of sequence it would have thrown everything off. This had to happen out of love, so that every deliverance today would be effective.

When doing deliverance, one must remember all that Jesus had to accomplish. I have access because it has been granted. Now, it is important to execute and remove the things that are unauthorized.

In Leviticus 14:53 the priest, (like Jesus Christ did later), would purify the house and make it ceremonially clean. Jesus had to fulfill this ceremonial cleaning to make sure that our rooms are clean. A contaminated house can be misleading; it can lead you to believe that it's not contaminated even though it is. If you don't think your house is contaminated, you will not call the priest. However, you still have to know if you are sick. So, what has Christianity done? It has told people that once they are saved, they are delivered. Therefore, when someone comes to the front of the church and repeats the "Salvation Prayer," it is assumed that they are free of all the things that mortify them. They go home thinking that everything is okay. On the contrary, to their surprise, certain bad habits remain, and they end up inheriting other foul spirits like guilt and culpability.

Jesus paid a high ransom so that it would not be so easy for us to go to hell. Deliverance is about cleaning your feet. Could the body be cleaned? (See John 13:1-17). Yes, it is salvation, but your feet continually get dirty. This statement derives from the conversation Jesus had with Peter in John chapter 13 when Jesus decided to wash the feet of His disciples. Peter first declined, because he felt himself unworthy. Jesus responded by telling him if he did not get his feet clean he would not belong to Him. This statement prompted Peter to blurt out and say, then wash my whole body. Jesus responded, you are already clean but your feet get continually dirty.

Here we see a picture of deliverance and how it is distinguished and separated from salvation. When you come to the Lord, you are washed by the blood of Jesus. However, your feet need to be continually washed because you are still walking on the earth. Hence, the reason why we must be mindful of each other's feet; that is deliverance.

Soul Ties, Blood Connections, and Transferences

During intimacy, there is an exchange that takes place. This becomes something that is inherited but does not belong to you. You could cut that curse but you have to know about it. You have to find out what strand it came from. A person could have a curse in their bloodline that could affect you. For example, if poverty is prevalent in that person's family, when unauthorized intimacy takes place you also inherit the poverty of that bloodline. God made it clear in Leviticus that life is in the blood, (Leviticus 16:15-16). This text demonstrates the usage of blood to purify and with this we find that life is in the blood.

According to the Word of God, sprinkling blood causes holiness. The priest would sprinkle the blood on the horns of the altar, causing holiness (Leviticus 16:18-19). Of course, today we know the blood was sprinkled on humanity by way of the cross.

If we look at it from another angle, the transference of blood can also be negative. In regards to tattoos, it is not the images that make it evil or wrong. It is the blood pact that takes place. That is why the satisfaction is not just the mark. The enemy prefers there to be a blood exchange. You are using the blood the same way it was used in the Old Testament, to establish a pact. Your blood is involved in the needle, so you end up inheriting what the blood pact signifies. The enemy makes you think that there isn't anything wrong, so people end up doing it even while assisting the church. They use Christian statements like: "I love Jesus," "The Lord is my Shepherd," and "Christ Rules." The statement being made is not the issue; it is the act of covenant that makes it wrong.

Transferences

When transferences take place, there are specifics that are required. The impartation took place when the priest would put his hands on the goat's head. The transference is now from the priest to the goat. The goat takes on all of the transgressions of the people and releases it into the wilderness. This is where the term *scapegoat* comes from. In definition, it means one who takes the blame of others. The laying of hands on a head is an exchange; someone is giving and someone is receiving, (Leviticus 16:20-22).

Transferences through Clothing

Earlier I mentioned the special Zadok priesthood and the anointing that even the clothes absorbed (Ezekiel 44:15-19). The anointing on the clothes was so strong that God said, make sure you put the clothing somewhere so that you do not hurt the people because there is too much holiness. I like to compare this to the moment when Jesus was walking towards healing Jairus' daughter. A woman looking for a solution to her sickness for the past 12 years went in an unauthorized manner (according to the Jewish law), touched His mantle and received her healing (Matthew 9:18-25). Her problem was greater than the situation, so she broke protocol to get to Jesus. She thought to herself, I'll touch Him even if it's just his mantle! The anointing on Jesus' clothing was a revelation she received. This was proven when virtue "power" was released from Jesus the moment she touched His robe.

The Importance of Praying Over Food

There are some pagan customs that have a spiritual connection, (Ezekiel 46:19-20). If you eat their traditional foods or any other cuisine that is connected to rituals and don't pray over the food, you end up taking in the transference of those rituals. You are not just praying for the food to be physically edifying, but also spiritually edible because they could be putting different levels of witchcraft in it. As long as you are here on earth, you have to deal with all of that.

If there is a puddle of mud and you are clean, but you decide to jump in, would you still be clean? No, but are you a Christian? Yes. It's not about being a Christian, it's about the natural order of things. God is always protecting us from us because we are always making mistakes. Therefore, He tries to set things up so that we can get out of our mess and not get in that mess again, (Ezekiel 6).

One of the practical examples I like to use is that of an electrical transformer. The electricity flowing is calibrated to enter into the homes without destroying and exploding the appliances. Without Jesus, we would not be able to deal with the raw flow of the anointing, the power of God. It could literally kill us. Our design is for earth. Jesus grants us access to Heaven and all that Heaven has to offer. That is why everything has to be done in His name. Yes, you can be endangered if too much holiness is given to you. Let us use Jesus as an example. He became the transformer where the electric flow would allow us to contain and distribute the right amount of power (Ezekiel 46:20 NLT).

Other Types of Transferences

In Romans, 10:17 it says that faith comes by hearing. There is transference in reading, speaking, singing, and touching. If faith comes by hearing, it is because somebody is speaking it. What has been spoken is transferred into your thought process.

Hearing

We are either giving or receiving. It is the nature of who we are. Information with toxins can be taken in or given in the same way. The enemy has always worked using the Trojan horse effect. He does not unveil his evilness right away, but rather allows you to celebrate a fake victory. What he has "within the gift" will come out at the time you are asleep. If you know the story of the Trojan Horse, then you understand the way you defeat is to enter in unsuspectedly. This can happen by songs, conversations, and seemly meaningless movements.

Reading and Speaking

Just like sound, when you are reading, you are placing an image to a text. In other words, we still receive in this manner. Therefore, the enemy will use words to infiltrate and create standards that are anti design.

Singing

When it comes to singing, there is a deeper embedment of seeds because the mind is not just taking in the words. Melody is creating another file in the archives of the mind. Now, something spoken once is now being repeated over and over just because of a melody. In music, the chorus is always repeated. That strategy is what the enemy uses to infiltrate the conscious and subconscious. When I was young, there was a song that spoke of killing the police. It was repeated over and over again in the chorus until it became part of the subconscious. This had a ripple effect that led a generation of people to be in opposition of those in law enforcement. The recipients of the message in this song experienced a melodious trap or a Trojan Horse effect.

Power of Laying on of Hands

In Acts chapter 8:4-25 we find an evangelist by the name of Philip who did a lot of miracles, signs, and wonders. He caught the attention of someone by the name of Simon the Sorcerer. Many people spoke of him as the great one or the power of God. When Simon saw that Philip was moving in supernatural powers, he started following the power and not the source of the power. His approach was to be his disciple for a little while. Then something happened. Jerusalem heard what Philip was doing so they sent Peter and John to investigate. Once they arrived, they prayed in the presence of Simon the sorcerer. When Peter and John laid hands upon those new believers, something supernatural took place. Whatever it was, it was something greater than what he had seen Philip do. According to the Word, Philip was casting out demons, and healing the sick.

However, when Simon saw all that Peter and John had done, he said, let me have this power too. He was even willing to pay for it. The demand to obtain what they had was stronger. If they were not healing or delivering those men, something physical must have happened to cause Simon to want to pay for it.

How do I know I am Free?

When you are changed by way of behavior modification, you are only moving in the right direction based on your own strength. When you are transformed, you are no longer attracted to what you were bound to. For example, when a person makes a conscious decision to stop drinking, their subconscious is still attracted to the alcohol. All it takes is a bad moment and they are back to drinking alcohol again. However, when you are transformed, your appetite is not the same. The alcohol now becomes repulsive. You no longer desire what the flesh wants because it does not appeal to you anymore.

Here is an illustration I like to use to explain this phenomenon: a caterpillar has the ability to change colors, so when it is on a green leaf it camouflages to green, when it's on the bark of a tree it camouflages to brown. In the world of the caterpillar, there would be a celebration of changing from one color to another. The truth is, it still has the same appetite. It still walks the same way, and it still views things the same way. Transformation is when a caterpillar enters into a stage of deliverance and becomes a butterfly. Once it is a butterfly, it no longer desires the same things. It does not look back to the leaf and reminisce of the moment when it indulged in it before. It has a completely different panoramic view on life: no longer walking, but now flying.

Forgiveness

So how do you know when you have been delivered? Your appetite, view, and walk have been completely transformed. You know you have forgiven someone when you can think of him or her and not feel repulsed by the person. Forgiveness is healing as well. It may seem as a choice, but as I mentioned earlier, "behavior modification" is different from "soul transformation." A person can decide to forgive but still be unwilling to forgive in their soul. They may say something like, "I forgive you, but I will not forget."

Although that may sound normal and plausible in the secular world, it demonstrates there are roots that still need deliverance.

Lack of forgiveness becomes an obstacle. It is also evidence the enemy uses against you in the courtroom of Heaven. As long as the enemy has evidence against you based on what you have against someone else, a door remains open for the enemy to cause an infraction against you. The enemy cannot move under his own concupiscence. He is still required to follow rules and regulations that are connected to the courtroom of Heaven.

At this point in the book, I would like to take a moment to help you pray if there is unforgiveness in your life so that you can be free. If you do not forgive, you place major limitations on your life. Forgiveness is the essence of

Christianity. In the natural order of things, there's "payback." That is the law "eye for an eye, tooth for a tooth." Jesus said turn the other cheek. The distinction between the world and the church is not the clothes you wear, or how long you pray. It is what you do in a moment like that. Do you want to distinguish yourself as a Christian? Is your Christianity based on a circumstance? What you do in your hardest moment is a determining factor to whether or not you are connected.

The measure of a person is not when things are good. It is when things are bad. We are dealing with principalities, and demonic realms. In other words, God is saying if you want to be part of this move in deliverance, then it is important for you to demonstrate that you can harness

something that can cause harm to someone and not release it
when you are upset.

God will not give you a gun unless you know who
the enemy is and how to use it. If you are led by emotions,
you are still looking at the person. You have not separated
the person from the things "demonic entities" that are
influencing them to behave in such a manner.

Forgiveness Prayer

Lord, we come before You acknowledging the open
door; You said in Your Word that You are the Lord. Today,
we cross over to the side where freedom is found in
abundance. Today, I remove the clothing of captivity, and I
allow all areas of my life to be inspected and cleaned by the
power of Holy Spirit.

Chapter 6

The Heavenly Court System

What is the Heavenly Court System?

In the court system, Jesus is our defense attorney, Holy Spirit is our Counselor, and God "the Father" is our judge. The devil is the accuser. Every day and every hour, there is a court case being held on your behalf. This is not the Great White Throne Judgment, but it holds the same type of weight to parallel your day-to-day activity.

To further explain, in the Book of Revelation chapter 4 we encounter a glimpse of the Heavenly Courtroom. We find a total of 24 elders, each one presiding in every hour of the day. We also find four living beings. Their job is to oversee occurrences that take place in every season. He who knows all and sees all is Holy Spirit. He is described in chapter 4 as the seven-fold spirit.

If you remove the numbers, you find that the courtroom is open 24 hours a day, 7 days a week within the 4 seasons. This description allows us to see how mindful God is. He is mindful, not just after we die, but actually, during the time we are alive.

Therefore, every time you lie, there is an infraction and the consequence is based on the level of infraction. It's like when you are driving on a highway in which the speed limit is 55 miles per hour. If you go 1 mile over the speed limit, law enforcement reserves the right to stop you. However, the consequence has to be parallel to the infraction. Simultaneously, in another situation, if you decide to go 90 miles an hour, the consequence is greater. Many people decide to go faster because the infraction does not stop you from breaking the law. That is why when we sin; we think we

got away with it since we did not see the immediate

consequence in the natural realm. The adversary waits just as

a traffic enforcer would wait to stop you. It is not worth it to

stop you for only 5 miles over the speed limit. The adversary

would rather wait until you are comfortable in your sin to

pull you over after you are significantly over your speed limit.

Your Words Activate the Heavenly Court System

There is another part of the Word that says there

was silence in Heaven for 30 minutes, (Revelation 8:1). This

demonstrates how important every moment is for God. In the

Courtroom there is power given to every word that is

released. This is one of the reasons for which we have

a right to remain silent and anything that we say may be held against us or used for us in the Courtroom of Heaven, based on what we see here on earth. The power of a decree and declaration activates the court system that brings divine justice or judgment. This is why it is important to make it a lifestyle to please God and not a methodology.

Defining justice and injustice is predicated on how much is revealed to the person standing in the place of judgment. As we all know, Jesus died on the cross and became a living sacrifice. This level of evidence holds much weight in the courtroom of heaven. Therefore, the only way the enemy can hold evidence against the person standing trial is by their lack of information.

Presenting your Case

In order to present your case effectively, you must know how to make decrees. Remind God of injustice committed. Petition and proclaim liberty. Everything presented has to be connected to what Jesus did on the cross. All evidence presented by the enemy must be filtered through the blood of Jesus. When presenting your case, you must be aware of pre-dispensational truths and post dispensational truths. In other words, utilize the Old Testament Scripture out of context for New Testament events.

An example that illustrates a difference between the Old Testament and the New Testament is when the Old Testament mentions the execution of children who are disrespectful to their parents.

This does not apply in the New Testament because what has been given is the power of transformation "deliverance." This now becomes an option when presenting your case in Heaven. So prior to the cross, the law had to be harsh to eliminate the cancer. However, after the cross, the solution has been granted by way of cleaning of the rooms. It is interesting that instead of removing the problem and rendering execution, the option now is to fix the problem by addressing the roots.

Sonship

There is a total of seven cases presented in the Heavenly Courtroom. In the courtroom, to know your identity is really important. Who you are, will determine your exoneration. Identity is not just important on earth; it is even more important in the spiritual realm.

Usually, the bloodline is a determining factor in distinguishing your connection to someone else. Life is in the blood and the identification is in the blood. The question we ask is why did Jesus have to shed His blood? One of the things that took place at the cross was a blood transfusion. So as a son and a daughter, you are acknowledged as a relative at the point of entry into the courtroom.

There is a point in the courtroom where you have to state your name, and because the Son is related to the Judge, we must show our relationship to the Son. In our identity, we find there are assignments that are connected to our functions. By receiving Jesus, we are now sons and daughters, not just creation. Our roles are now heightened and connected to the ultimate purpose. We have become the original complete design of ministry. Once you are part of the perfect design of God, you are given a function to help advance the kingdom and spiritually mature the church. That function is within one of the five-fold ministries. They are the apostolic, prophetic, evangelistic, pastoral or teacher.

The role of Jesus has always been to reconcile the disqualifications of humanity. Holy Spirit empowers us but our identity is in the name of Jesus and the authorization is by the Father.

In the courtroom, while Jesus speaks to the Father on our behalf, Holy Spirit speaks to us at the same time. He helps us to remain silent and be at peace even when we have the urge to defend ourselves. "Be still, and know that I am God!" (Psalm 46:10 NLT). We have a choice of paying attention to the accuser or the counselor "Holy Spirit" since both are speaking at the same time.

The Devil Needs Evidence

Just like here on earth, the burden of ***proof*** is placed on the prosecutor. In other words, the prosecutor is required to present evidence to accuse the person on trial. Simultaneously, the defender also has to present proof of exoneration, regardless of how egregious the crime might be.

The Proof of our Freedom Lies on the Blood Stained Hands of Jesus

While we remain silent, Jesus speaks on our behalf. However, the moment we speak on our behalf, He becomes silent and allows us to speak. His silence has everything to do with respecting our choice hence **freewill**. Our freedom is in His voice and not in ours.

My Testimony as an Example

My experience in the courtroom is actually very personal. I have been made privy to its functionality, since I was accused and found guilty of a crime. My experience in the courtroom was extremely arduous. Especially watching those I love go through the same roller-coaster ride I was going through. I paid attention to the movements of the judge, the sidebars of the attorneys and the back and forth of the jury. I became a witness and recipient of a watered down heavenly court session. This very revelation obligates me to share with you that even if you are not punished for a past crime, if not addressed, it will appear as evidence in the courtroom.

There is a difference with being super optimistic and moving in faith. Super optimism declares a false sense of security based on not being caught. Faith is a true expression of facing your past crimes with the hope of exoneration. In my case, I was more into super optimism until that day came. It all caught up to me. I thought because I was consecrated to the Lord that I did not have to pay the price for something I did in the past. I felt leaving the Real Estate industry altogether was enough. I found out very fast this is not how the courtroom functions. My transition was precarious. As I began to move in the ministry, I thought that was sufficient to be absolved of a "white-collar crime" that took place six years earlier. God had other plans. I am grateful for that penal system "college". Without it, I would have never graduated or received the revelation that I have today.

When people say, "I am washed by the ***Blood*** of Jesus and all the things that I have done are no longer held against me," there is a level of truth to that. However, keep in mind that there is also a present and future situation that needs to be exonerated. This is not for ***salvation*** but rather for ***deliverance***. When Jesus died on the cross, He died for our sins, and gave us access to Heaven. Most of us just look towards the cross for ***salvation***. However, while He was there, He opened the door for peace while we are alive and healing for our bodies. Our entry into Heaven is not the issue. Walking presently in a type of hell is.

Jesus Said, "It is finished!"

In (John 19:30 NIV), it is written that Jesus said, "It is finished." By that statement, Jesus meant that everything, which needed to be revealed, was revealed. Whether or not you catch that revelation is up to you. So there is a revelation of salvation, a revelation of deliverance, and a revelation of healing. They need to be understood if we are to be a participant of each one. You can repent of your sins and still have doors open. Repentance without full revelation of what you are repenting for is incomplete.

You Can Be saved, but not Delivered and Healed

Salvation is based on a heart condition, not a flesh condition. Salvation leads to the healing and perfecting of the soul and flesh; some would call it sanctification. Deliverance is not obtainable if the healing of the soul is not complete. "…who, by the power that enables him to bring everything under his control, will transform our lowly bodies so that they will be like his glorious body" (Philippians 3:21 NIV).

In John 5, when he speaks of the lame man, he states that Jesus did not ask the man if he wanted to be healed. Jesus asked him if he wanted to be made whole. In addition, the thief on the cross was not delivered. He acknowledged who Jesus was and simply due to that acknowledgment, he was the first to walk into paradise under the new covenant. The last shall be first and the first shall be last. He was the last in the ministry of Jesus and the first to enter.

Meanwhile, the patriarchs of the Old Testament entered last, even though they were first.

Generational Curses

We know that in the medical field there are diagnoses that are concluded by identifying who the family members are and whether or not they have had any type of sicknesses or diseases. If you have ever been to the hospital, you know that the first thing they will ask you is if someone in your family has a certain type of sickness. In the case of Cancer, it is quite probable that if it runs rampant in your family, you can easily become a potential recipient of that vital disease.

If there is someone on their deathbed and their reason for being there is Cancer, it is understood that if they accepted the Lord on a Sunday but died of that same disease on a Monday, they still have a passage to heaven. We would accept that faster than accepting the fact that someone could have Cancer in their soul even though they accepted Jesus as their Savior.

We are not a social club, or fraternal order and we are not a gang. The rule of entry is not based on our interpretation of who qualifies and who does not. Our job is to offer the truth and become ministers of reconciliation. If the person does not get it, we are not authorized to kick them out. We keep working with them until they are able to get it right. If we do it in love, then we can rest assured that our present love is stronger than their past behavior, especially since our love is connected to the love of God.

AIDS?

AIDS is the consequence of an act. There are also victims who had nothing to do with the act, but had to pay the consequence of the act (children born with AIDS). If a person on his/her deathbed with AIDS dies, but received the Lord Jesus as their Savior prior to death, we easily accept they did it. However, things are different if someone dies of a mental illness like depression but accepted Jesus as their Lord.

Just like the sickness of AIDS, the depression didn't go away. The application of deliverance had not been done. If you can believe the person who died with AIDS could go to Heaven, it should not be hard to believe that the person who accepted Christ the day before they died of depression also went to Heaven.

Some People Are not Mentally Capable

In an earthly courtroom it is clear when someone is not functioning in their full capacity (ability or power to do, experience, or understand something) or not using their full faculties (inherent mental or physical powers), it is considered by the judge in the area of judgment and sentencing. If we were to put to trial the man in Mark 5 who was in the cemetery breaking chains, yelling, and running around in the nude, at first glance, we would think this person needs time in prison. However, Jesus saw this was a soul issue. In the courtroom of Heaven, what we need to present is healing in the soul. If we apply the same scenario today, sanity is defined as being able to distinguish good and bad according to the general populous. Just like Jesus, we need to look beyond the surface and not be quick to condemn. Only He knows the heart and the heart condition of the person.

Homosexuality and Deliverance

You can be delivered and healed but not saved. What I am about to bring to the forefront is a bit controversial. The Lord has allowed me to experience a small portion of His love for humanity. I know His desire to save, deliver, and heal all creation is paramount. Homosexuality is a hot topic today. Many that have taken on the title of healers have turned into executioners. What are we doing about this problem? Are we depending on methods and behavioral modification or are we trusting the transforming love of God to bring them out of that stage or ailment?

If a homosexual person sincerely receives the Lord Jesus Christ as their Savior, but the next day still finds themselves attracted to the same behaviors and while being under that attraction ends up losing their life, was their acceptance of Jesus the day before strong enough to outdo their present decrepit condition? Would that be considered the same as someone who dies of a disease one day but accepted the Lord on another?

The anointing is always looking for an area to fix. A person who is anointed, when connected to someone else, is a part of the solution and not a part of the problem. Again, we are called ministers of reconciliation and not ministers of condemnation.

So ultimately, what do I believe? I believe the Judgment Throne is too big for us to sit on and regardless what the infraction, we are not in position to determine someone's destiny. The Bible says we must repent of ours sins and not live a lifestyle congruent to our former self. Some deliverances can happen instantly, but there are others that require time. "Don't copy the behavior and customs of this world, but let God transform you into a new person by changing the way you think. Then you will learn to know God's will for you, which is good and pleasing and perfect" (Romans 12:2 NLT).

Prior to that, you cannot know what is good, pleasing, and perfect. Notice that it says let God transform you. It does not say modify yourself. Only then, do you know what God's will is for you. What I am saying is that I am using the same concept as the Passover. God will deal with you in your process, but that has nothing to do with your salvation. Salvation, deliverance, and healing are different.

At what point is your mind transformed? Do you believe that receiving Jesus as Lord and Savior and then being transformed is also a process? People believe that salvation and deliverance are the same. When you come to accept the Lord as your Savior, you are okay now. You go back home after receiving Jesus, but you are still angry, you still want to drink alcohol, and do all types of drugs.

Prior to that alcohol or drug issue, you came to God and said, "Lord I want to be free," and He says, you are saved! Now I stamp you, I place my seal of approval over you since all you had to do was accept me. Then we keep adding things to the list of John 3:16. What is it that is required?

To believe! Believing leads to transformation because you cannot stay the same way you are anymore. If you die the day after you received Jesus as Lord and Savior, do you mean to tell me that because your process was not complete you are going to hell?

Do you mean to tell me that a homosexual who goes to church, receives the Lord, and says, "here I am" with tears in his eyes, is already transformed? What if they die the next day? Are you going to condemn them to hell? Transformation may require more time. I am not telling you that in some cases you will not be transformed. I am telling you that the general populous believe that people require time for transformation.

The man on the cross caught a revelation. He was not delivered yet. He recognized who Jesus was. He caught the revelation, but he did not catch the deliverance yet.

Jesus said, because you caught the revelation this day, you will be with me in paradise.

Suicide

Suicides were considered hell bound. Today you have people that say, "Yes they went to hell because they took their lives!" What you do not know is that person may have had something missing which caused them to be sick. Think of the person who dies of cancer on Monday having accepted the Lord on Sunday.

The first thing people ask is, "did they do the Sinners Prayer?" If that is also applicable to someone who dies of a soul cancer called depression, is that also acceptable? I am aware of people who repeat the Sinners Prayers just on sound, like a parrot that hears a sound and repeats without an understanding of the essence of the message. The same occurs when some people repeat the Salvation Prayer without capturing the essence.

What about a person who is internally sick, living a life of depression? The enemy has that person tied down; depressed all day long until one day that depression takes the person to a point where they take pills and overdose. Some people would say, "I don't know if that person made it to Heaven." How do you know and who are you to know? Since when do you sit comfortably on the Throne of God? Do your feet stay dangling when you are sitting there? Surely, your feet cannot touch the ground since you are unauthorized to sit on the Throne of God and make a statement like that. Unfortunately, condemnation and desertion seem to be the desired approach for many groups.

Heavenly Court Case of Jesus

We know that Jesus endured one of the most horrific moments that a human can endure. Although the focus is always on His passion or physical pain, there is a lot more going on. Due to the fact that Jesus was a citizen of Heaven and earth, He paved the way and stood trial in front of Himself in the courtroom of Heaven while being on trial on earth. According to the author of Hebrews, He had to fulfill both the roles of "High Priest" and "Sacrifice." Therefore, in a courtroom setting, we are looking at Him as both judge and accused since Jesus is the only person in the universe able to speak effectively on His own behalf. There was no need for a lawyer. While He was on trial, He spoke the language of the judge. He knew all the legal codes and was able to address the prosecutor. While He remained silent on earth, He spoke volumes in Heaven.

Now, when I am talking about dual citizenship I am referring to both levels of understanding. This is why when Jesus spoke you have to determine whether He was speaking about matters of earth or Heaven. One classic example we find is in John 5 where Jesus refers to Himself as receiving all authority and making the final judgment over everything. Then, a few verses later, He makes a statement that seems contradictive. He says all power comes from the Father. He does all things and He makes all things by way of His Father's permission. In this, we see His dual citizenship where He spoke in Kairos and then later spoke in Chronos, while standing trial on earth. It may have seemed as if He was weak and disorientated, however, the stance that was being made for the well-being of the universe, was unfolding. While He stood in front of Pontius Pilate, He also stood in front of Himself as the Father. Therefore, silence on earth is noise in Heaven. That is why prayer is so powerful. Although you are in your most vulnerable position on earth, you are moving mountains in the spiritual realm.

If we were to take a snap shot picture of Jesus in the heavenly courtroom during His trial, it would look like this: Jesus would be the Judge, the defense attorney, the counselor and the one on trial. The only two areas that would not apply to Him would be as prosecutor and jury. The reason for this chapter is so that we can understand that Jesus Himself already establishes our deliverance as case law. Before humanity was put on trial, He was placed on trial. The pattern He left was so eventually we would resurrect like He resurrected.

God Makes You Live What You Will Use as Revelation

There are many kingdom principles and in order to fully understand what they are, there may be a need for us to go through the process. This truth can be connected to what Jesus did according to the Book of John, "For I have come down from heaven not to do my will but to do the will of Him who sent me" (John 6:38 NIV). In doing so, He established case laws on earth and for Heaven. Heaven can now say that it is aware of all of the levels and conditions of humanity. Jesus expanded the library of Heaven; where before it was as Creator to created. After His three and a half years of ministry, He expanded the library with human experiences, not just by witnessing, but also doing. God's expression of compassion was limited because He was at His throne, but once He became man, He was able to assimilate all levels of pain and hurt. This is why His desire to heal increased after the cross. Judgment was satisfied and no longer did you hear about God wiping out whole villages and towns, because Jesus had reconciled the wrath and confusion between Heaven and earth.

The Courtroom of Heaven, the Different Stages: Kingship, Priesthood, Life, Death, Destiny, Paternal and Inheritance

There are many kinds of courts here on earth that can be compared to the Courtroom of Heaven. Supreme Court, Civil Court, Family Court, and Appellate Court are just some earthly examples of the types of cases that are presented in the Heavenly Court.

The Courtroom of Heaven

The Courtroom of Heaven has allowed you to speak and not be afraid, not of men, the devil or demons. At the end of the day, you have grace. The grace that is upon your life, you want to use now, not later.

Do you want to wait until you die to use your grace? Do not just use it as a passage to get to Heaven! Use it now! Eventually you will get to Heaven, but I am telling you that you have it now.

The Revelation of Salvation, Deliverance and Healing

Salvation is one thing, deliverance is another, and Healing is another. Each one of those three stages has its purpose. If you think that they are all one thing, there is a need to re-assess. Some people think that someone on a wheelchair should be able to walk the moment they are saved. Others say the moment they are saved they should be transformed, and the moment you are saved you should be healed.

Jesus did say, "...It Is Finished...", (John 19:30 NLT). What is finished? You are saved. You can be delivered. You can be healed. As I mentioned before, it is possible for someone to be saved and not delivered. Is it possible to be saved and not be healed? If I am really saved and not healed, then why is it impossible for me to be saved and not delivered? The difference here is that, if you are saved and not delivered, you have Heaven in your future but hell in your present.

When you are saved, your salvation is the determining factor that you have your mansion and your mansion is secured. If you are living poor in spirit here, it's because you do not want to believe that there is an area of healing internally that needs to take place. You are satisfied with your situation and you say: "Don't worry, my mansion is in Heaven. I don't mind being broke now." That is you. I do not receive that! I believe that God has given us the five breads and two fish season NOW! Now is the time where He is going to produce a lot. We have to change our paradigms and not be satisfied. Even the person who is sick can either stay there or say "No!"

My salvation gives me access to my healing. Better than that, my salvation gave me access to my soul being healed by which my body responds. Some people are sick not because their bodies are producing sickness. They are sick as a manifestation of their soul. The manifestation of their soul is what is keeping them sick. Something in this area has not been opened up yet. God is saying, I want to heal your soul so that you can walk again. I want to heal your soul so that you can live again. I don't want you to be like Lazarus who was alive but still bound. I need you to know that I care about you being free. Don't be satisfied with just being alive and breathing. Be free and free indeed.

There are things in the Bible that we need to rightly divide. A lot of us go by verses. We take a verse, take it out of context, stretch it until it turns into something else, and make a denomination out of it. If you don't know the Word or why things are happening historically during biblical times, ask Holy Spirit to grant you insight on post and pre-dispensational truths.

The Legal System of Heaven

All charges against you have been dropped. What was nailed on the cross was everything you would ever do. The cross is so that we could sit where we are. The cross is so we may continue walking. He died to live. It was an intentional death. He took His own life to live on purpose. He committed Holy suicide.

Legal Rights

When we talk, gossip, doubt, express jealously, anxiety, worry, envy, speak negative and actually move in these areas, you allow the enemy to use evidence against you in the Courtroom of Heaven. Even after a prayer service where you were strongly connected with the Spirit of God. If you decide to start murmuring and gossiping afterwards, you move away from the purpose and assignment of God and immediately give access to the enemy.

The Gospel is Inclusive, not Exclusive

Most people, by nature, want everyone to go through whatever they went through; almost like a rite of passage. However, Jesus made it clear that whatever He went through was so that we would not go through it.

Chapter 7

Rules of Engagement

In ancient times, the rules of engagement were clear and honored by both sides of the fence. When conducting deliverance, these rules of engagement apply. The enemy continues to gain ground as long as you are not able to declare or decree a revelation that puts a stop to his demand.

When Jesus was in the desert, these rules of engagement were clear. While the devil was trying to tempt Jesus, He spoke words that repelled and thwarted the enemy's strategies. The way the enemy engages is also part of his nature. While Jesus presents Himself with the sword, which is indicative to His nature of close proximity, the enemy prefers to shoot arrows and darts from afar. Most archers, when selected, one of the areas that distinguish them is their fear of hand to hand combat. This is why I am a firm believer of using the Word as a sword and not the shooting of arrows.

Jesus Rebuked the Wind

The meaning of the word rebuke is to reprimand or correct. When you rebuke a child, you are not casting them out. We have been taught that we are to rebuke a demon and that is it. There is more to it. You must cast out the demon because rebuking is correcting. In (Mark 4:39 NLT) we read that Jesus rebuked the wind: "When Jesus woke up, he rebuked the wind and said to the waves, 'Silence! Be still!' Suddenly the wind stopped, and there was a great calm." In order to rebuke something or someone, there has to be understanding. In other words, the wind needed to understand, and it did have that ability.

The Region of the Gerasenes

In the region of the Gerasenes (Mark 5:1-20) Jesus knew He would meet with a man who was possessed. The possession was complete; held by the enemy. Jesus did not even speak aloud but the demons knew He had said something. They asked, "Why do you torture us?" Jesus asked the things (meaning the demons), "What is your name?" And the response was: "My name is Legion." He went from being singular (my) to being many (legion). Jesus had already dealt with the principality, so the demon was weak. This made it easier to deal with that particular legion. The religious spirit and the spirit of the Pharisees by way of the modern day *Sanhedrin* has caused the Northeastern province of the United States to fall under a category of judgment.

There are people living in poverty because of a religious spirit and people living in sickness, accepting their sickness because of this same spirit. I want to be clear on this; God does not inflict pain, sickness and diseases on anyone. However, if it occurs, He uses it for growth and for His glory (See John 9). Once you deal with the principality, everything else the enemy tries to do, falls apart.

Remember, the man found in the cemetery was possessed by demons. Simultaneously, in that region they were selling and herding pigs. Since the law of the land forbade people from eating pigs, it opened up a window for the individual as well as the people in that region.

The Wind as Principality or Individual as Principality

Adolf Hitler in Germany was the instrument of the principality of that region. As long as he was alive, the principality in the atmosphere was strong against Jews. He was the embodiment. Once he was killed, everyone felt guilt. The principality was functioning through a person in that region. There are footages of people crying, afterwards, of guilt and remorse for accepting the Nazi propaganda against the Jews. These are the same people that said it's okay for them to die. The reason for which they did this was because they were under a stronghold witchcraft.

Saddam Hussein is another example of a Principality

Another example of a person being the object of connection with a principality was Saddam Hussein. He caused everyone in that region to rise up. He caused people to want to fight and rebel. Once he was executed, that principality had to connect to someone else, and that next victim was the embodiment of terrorism, Osama Bin Laden. He had to be killed because he was the incarnation of evil in that region. Once he was gone, that principality was no longer empowered, based on that assignment of worldwide terrorism.

Stipulations of Deliverance in a Nutshell

The stipulations of deliverance are: (a) target the atmosphere that includes authorities and principalities, (b) call on Heavenly assistance (the Angelic), separate the person from the things (meaning spiritual oppressors), (c) self-inventory: identify what is inside the person, what is there (d) be mindful of not losing your compassion, (e) sever generational curses: by way of renouncing and identifying the generational strongholds, such as poverty, addiction, sexual immorality, and other things, (f) always identify that God is the source of all the power, and (g) as you remove, also remember to put back in (love, joy, faith, peace, happiness, and other similar fruits of the spirit).

Glimpse of Deliverance

Visible signs of a person being delivered include: demons exit through sweat, tears, coughing, vomit, gas, shaking. Shaking is not always indicative of Holy Spirit filling in a person. Sometimes, it may be the person manifesting.

The War against Angels and Demons: Know your Rights as a Deliverance Minister and Become Untouchable while Conducting Deliverance

In regards to the angelic and demonic, there is a lot that can be written. The epic battle between the light and darkness can be seen when conducting deliverance.

In Hebrews chapter 1 it is clear that angels are assigned to believers. However, what you do and how you involve them is a whole other story. Angels were created to always desire to serve. Unlike humans who always want something in return, angels are always in anticipation of receiving an order. Before every deliverance, I thank God for their participation and I give them instructions. The acknowledgment of their involvement plays a major role in how successful deliverances are. One of the greatest examples of what I am referring to, regarding the angels' involvement in deliverance took place recently.

What happened was that a young woman was consumed with her previous lifestyle in sexual immorality. As we proceeded in identifying the problem, the angelic were used in taunting those foul spirits that were tormenting this young woman. Before I continue, I will inform the reader that my mother worked in microbiology as a lab technician and based on my exposure to her endeavor, I will be able to explain the events that took place.

In the body, there are bad and good cells. The bad cells are promoting their propaganda to try to influence other cells to be bad. Simultaneously, there are good cells that desire to preach the gospel and convert other cells to be good. This young woman had a lot of bad cells in her, and deliverance is about speaking the good news and empowering the good cells to rebel against the propaganda of the bad cells. Deliverance doesn't just work with verbiage; you must visualize spiritually what is going on.

In the military there is something called logistical lines
and it is a known fact that if you sever the supply lines
of the enemy, you cut the life source and limit their
propaganda (the angelic help to propel this objective in the
spiritual realm). I remember that many years ago during the
invasion of Iraq, one of the first things the United States did
was to cut all resources so that there would not be any
regrouping. This allowed me to see that the earthly tactics did
not start on earth, but rather between angels and demons in
the spiritual realm.

Angels are bold, but always need to be sent. They do
not move under their own instructions. On the other hand,
the demonic are always moving unauthorized. It is our job to
read to them our legal rights and present to them an eviction
notice stamped by the blood of Jesus. Angels work
accordingly, and follow the lead of a man or woman of God.

Remember they do not take orders from us, but rather from He who lives in us.

While many people claim to have seen an actual angelic body in a human body, (See Book of Hebrews), in deliverance, my exposure has been by way of black dots and multi-color bright lights. I know when angels are around and I know when demons are around. My involvement in this ministry for so many years has allowed me to detect them and the immediate reaction of their presence. However, there have been several times when, from the face of the person, another face would surface. This is why it is important to separate the things from the person.

As I mentioned before, there is so much more that can be written on this topic and is the reason why I intend to write a book directed to the "Angelic and Demonic" activity during deliverance.

The "Keys" of Deliverance to the Kingdom Have Been Granted

The Heavenly court system allows you to walk in with your chest and head high. The enemy's tactic has been to make you feel so guilty that you don't show up. "I will give him the key to the house of David—the highest position in the royal court. When he opens doors, no one will be able to close them; when he closes doors, no one will be able to open them" (Isaiah 22:22 NLT). "And I will give you the keys of the kingdom of heaven, and whatever you bind on earth will be bound in heaven, and whatever you loose on earth will be loosed in heaven" (Matthew 16:19 NKJV).

Integrity of a Person Who is Going To Do Deliverance

There is a spiritual grid that is not like the grid that we are used to on earth. The verticals and horizontals are different and the way the enemy can see you is not the way we are used to identifying each other on earth. He is only able to see you when you display his authorship because he is the father of lies. In order to identify your location, you need to express that which is already connected to him. In other words, he cannot see light. There are ministers that are attempting to conduct deliverance while they are in grave need of it themselves. The number one disqualifier is unforgiveness. Any minister not moving in the ministry of reconciliation is putting both himself and the recipient in danger.

If we were to look at it through the courtroom of Heaven, everything that is in agreement with the enemy becomes evidence used before the deliverer and the person being delivered. The biblical example that many connect with is in Acts 19 (Seven sons of Sceva). These young men thought the power came through incantation (vain repetition). In turn, they received a rude awakening. According to the Word, they were badly beaten and all seven of them ran away in the nude trying to find refuge. I urge all who enter the ministry of Deliverance to be mindful of their own rooms that are contaminated and need cleaning.

Physical Sickness vs. Internal Sickness

We tend to gear more towards the physical, when we define sickness. When someone walks into a church with a physical terminal illness, we pray for him or her to be healed. If they are not healed, we do not question their salvation or their place in heaven. On the other hand, if someone comes in with an internal sickness that is not visible (depression, anxiety, or addiction), we immediately expect a change. If it does not happen, they are condemned to hell.

Soul sicknesses are a lot more prevalent than physical illnesses, but our grace is more towards the one who looks sick, versus the ones who are internally sick. To explain this point, I will go a little deeper and provide an example of what I am talking about.

Consider that on a Sunday, a man who uses a wheelchair enters church and receives Jesus as his Lord and Savior. If he dies of his physical sickness on Monday, we easily conclude the person obtained eternal life. However, if another person enters the church and accepts the Lord as a Savior, but suffers from depression and the very next day dies of an overdose due to a depression based on a drug addiction, we quickly enter the realm of condemnation, ascertaining the person did not make the cut (did not go to Heaven).

Salvation and deliverance are two separate things. Salvation is a free gift that does not need to be worked for. Meanwhile, deliverance requires a transformation of the soul by someone of spiritual authority who is able to remove what is binding the person.

Salvation Prayer

My God, today I stand in Your presence receiving my identity as your son/daughter. I receive Your representation in the courtroom of Heaven where I have already been declared innocent by the power of Your Blood and Your Resurrection. My life from this day forward is in Your hands. Do with me, as you will. I accept my assignment in the name of Jesus the Christ.

God wants you to be saved. Remember that in (Romans 10:9 NKJV) it is written: "...that if you confess with your mouth the Lord Jesus and believe in your heart that God has raised Him from the dead, you will be saved."

Also keep in mind the following words spoken by Jesus (John 3:16 NLT) when He said, "For this is how God loved the world: He gave his one and only Son, so that everyone who believes in him will not perish but have eternal life."

The Flow from the Throne Prayer

Lord, I connect with Your heart that is for everyone to participate in Your grace and just as the rain and sun (that do not distinguish by way of behavior), I ask that Your anointing that destroys the yolk, will fall upon the righteous and unrighteous, those who are lovable and unlovable. I present this case in the courtroom of Heaven so that every enemy that rises up will forget my name and remember Yours.

I speak new paradigms, and new wineskins to be able to retain the new wine. This, I declare by the authority of God the Father in the name of Jesus Christ His son, and by the power of His Holy Spirit. Amen.

The words expressed above remind me of (Isaiah 61:1-2 NIV), where it is written: "The Spirit of the Sovereign LORD is on me, because the LORD has anointed me to proclaim good news to the poor. He has sent me to bind up the brokenhearted, to proclaim freedom for the captives and release from darkness for the prisoners, to proclaim the year of the LORD's favor and the day of vengeance of our God, to comfort all who mourn..."

About the Author

Since 1998, Apostle Israel Peña has dedicated his life to spreading the Good News. In 2014, alongside his wife, Prophetess Dalimar Peña, they founded the Flow Kingdom Ministries.

As true spiritual parents, their passion for the empowerment and betterment of people of all cultures and backgrounds, is a trait that can be seen in the children of the house. Their obedience to the apostolic and prophetic call on their lives, ensures the continuance of the vision God has granted them for generations to come.

Apostle Peña is the Senior Pastor of The Flow Kingdom Ministries, located in the Bronx, New York. A

native of New York City, Apostle Peña has served diligently
in ministry since the late 1990's. Apostle Peña has been a
Senior Pastor since 2004 and presently oversees churches
within the States of New York, Connecticut, Florida, and
Kenya, Africa.

Throughout the years of overseeing churches,
Apostle Peña has a proven ability to foster relationships with
ministries in and outside of the United States, and with
fellow congregants within the churches that he oversees.
Apostle Peña is most fulfilled when helping people grow
spiritually. His vision and ability to nurture relationships lead
to long-term solutions and success.

Presently, the mission of his ministry, The FLOW
Kingdom Ministries is to unite Christians of common mind
to enter into concepts of the kingdom. To encourage growth
and edification within the church body, to promote spiritual

connection with God and others, to assist in the aims and purposes of the region, and to inspire growth in the areas of the fivefold ministry.

Apostle Peña believes in the transformative power of Holy Spirit and with God's anointing, he ministers to the people to experience the fullness of Holy Spirit by way of deliverance. He is committed on saving souls for Christ, and equips the leadership with practical and vital strategies of evangelism for today's generation. Furthermore, Apostle Peña serves as a Regional Director and Coordinator for United Chaplains State of New York and United Chaplain State of Connecticut. He also sits at the table for the New York Clergy Criminal Justice Task Force.